Dear Person Who has Had E

Trust. The hardest part of my story of being a compulsive gambler is trust. Mainly trusting myself. I have relapsed too many times to count. I have won thousands of dollars to only put it all back in the slot machine and then head over to the ATM to take out even more. When confronted by others, it was actually physically painful to tell the truth. I stole. I borrowed. I came up with all kinds of stories where I was somehow a victim. I did not trust myself. I still don't.

My husband forgave me numerous times. I have accepted that he still doesn't trust me fully, and honestly he shouldn't. I don't even know if I could have been forgiving if I were put in the same situation as him.

I sat through hundreds of meetings and had a number of conversations with gamblers who had a spouse, significant other, family or friend who simply had enough. Although I understand it comes to a point where you must protect yourself, I do know the worst thing for a compulsive gambler is to be alone. It must come down to who you know that person to be deep down without gambling. Because the addict is just point blank a liar and cannot be trusted.

So how does healing and forgiving begin? I know you have had enough. I know you do not want to keep going through this. I know your finances and credit are probably a mess. I know you think you cannot be with someone you cannot trust. I know your relationship is broken. I have been there. My husband has been there.

My advice would be take a good hard look at the gambler and try ridiculously hard to remove betrayal, lies and even finances. Don't forget them, just temporarily remove them from the equation. Are you able to still love that person? If yes, make a commitment to just love that person and-

- Work the program with them.
- Set limits and expectations.
- Set boundaries for moving forward.
  - My husband set an expectation that I would attend meetings at least once a week;
  - I was not allowed to have a debit card. My entire paychecks went in a joint account;
  - I was to have no credit cards (which didn't matter because my credit was destroyed);
  - I was to be completely honest no matter how painful it was.

If on the contrary you feel the love is not there and have truly had enough, my only advice is to give it time. Give the gambler an opportunity to show you who they once were. You may find they are an even better than before (if they are working the Gambler's Anonymous program).

I wrote 'Step Up" to assist the compulsive gambler with their 12 step program. I am now providing "Step In" to assist the loved ones of the compulsive gambler. I am tailoring the steps to provide guidance in helping you to "Step In" the thoughts of a compulsive gambler and heal not only your relationship, but yourself.

I will share stories of relationships that have been mended. I will share stories of giving up. I will share my husband and I's ups and downs through the years. I truly pray you find healing in your relationship.

"God, grant me the serenity to accept the things I cannot change, The courage to change the things I can, And the wisdom to know the difference."

STEP 1

We admitted we were powerless over gambling - that our lives had become unmanageable.

DEAR LOVED ONE: Has your loved one admitted this? Are they realizing they need help? Have they found help through gambler's anonymous? There is help for them. It may be that you are part of their inspiration to get help. If they have no reason to get help, they won't. It is not your responsibility to make that person get help. Your responsibility is to identify what you need to forgive.

There was a woman who came to meetings whose husband had moved out. He did not divorce her, but made it clear to her that he could not live with her until she got help. The decision was hers. He came with her to her first meeting and shared what he had been through. She had gone so far to pawn items from their home. He cried. He said he loved her but he could not trust her. She cried and came to an understanding she would lose him if she didn't get help. I am not certain how this developed, but her husband made a decision that protected him, and motivated her to get help.

Ephesians 9:32 Be kind and compassionate to one another, forgiving each other, just as in Christ God forgave you." "For if you forgive other people when they sin against you, your heavenly Father will also forgive you." "Bear with each other and forgive one another if any of you has a grievance against someone.

Make an inventory of what you love about the compulsive gambler?

_____

_____

_____

_____

_____

_____

What things can you simply not tolerate?

_____

_____

_____

_____

_____

_____

Make a list of expectations?

_____

_____

_____

_____

_____

_____

STEP 2

Came to believe that a Power greater than ourselves could restore us to a normal way of thinking and living.

DEAR LOVED ONE: Do you believe in God? Do you believe God can restore your gambler? Do you believe God can restore your relationship? Do you believe God can restore your finances? Do you pray?

My husband and I have always gone to church. We raised our kids in the church. We are very good at making our lives look very shiny, but we have encountered some pretty dark times. Even though we both believed in God, we never really prayed together. It felt uncomfortable. In the beginning of my recovery, I had accepted that God was going to help me, but I didn't know if my husband had accepted that. I started reading scripture and books on healing and forgiveness. I began to write on note cards passages I felt spoke to us directly. I began putting these note cards in his car, in his lunch, by his phone, etc. He kept them. So even though praying together seemed hard, this was my way of praying with my husband.

Praying together is easier for some, but not for all and that is okay. Your relationship with God can be very personal. But pray for your loved one. Pray for your relationship. If you don't know what to pray, just pray the serenity prayer on page 3. Prayer and hope in God is the key ingredient to recovery and restoration.

The Bible commands us to pray for one another, "Therefore, confess your sins to one another and pray for one another, that you may be healed. The prayer of a righteous person has great power as it is working" (James 5:16, ESV). God manifests Himself in many ways when praying together and for each other.

Are you ready to let God work in your lives? What are some things you can do to let him do that?

_____
_____
_____
_____
_____
_____
_____
_____

What are some things you can meditate on when you feel hopeless or impatient?

_____
_____
_____
_____
_____
_____
_____

How do you think God speaks to you?

_____

_____

_____

_____

_____

_____

STEP 3

**Made a decision to turn our will and our lives over to the care
of this Power of our own understanding.**

DEAR LOVED ONE: One of the hardest parts in my relationship
with my husband, was when he would keep bringing it up. This is
going to be a hard one. Hopefully by now, you have made a list of
your expectations and everything is confessed and out on the table.
There will be days when you want to lash out and remind that person
how they destroyed your life. There will be days when you want
that person to feel terrible about what they have done. My husband
still brings up stuff that happened 20 years ago. It is going to take
every bit of self control at times to not do this. This is where you
need to just give it to God to handle. God wants to prune us, and
that can be painful, but his ultimate goal is to make us better, wiser
and humble. Your loved one is trying to get there. Give it a chance.
Starting over at Step 1 repeatedly is not beneficial to their recovery.

When we **repent** *and turn back to Him, He forgives us and
cleanses us from all unrighteousness (1 John 1:9).*

What in your relationship would you like to see better?

_____

_____

_____

_____

_____

_____

_____

What do you believe your loved one needs to do to increase trust?

_____

_____

_____

_____

_____

_____

_____

What do you believe you need to do to forgive?

_____

_____

_____

_____

_____

_____

_____

STEP 4

Made a searching and fearless moral and financial inventory of ourselves.

DEAR LOVED ONE: Your loved one know what they did wrong. Your loved one knows. If they are not admitting this in their own step work, you might need to stay here a while. This is not about you reminding them about how morally flawed they are. In fact, they may not even want to share this with you. Our flaws can be very shameful. Your loved one may be struggling with why they have such integrity issues. Did those issues exist before the gambling, or did gambling cause them? You must focus on your own morality, and honestly, supporting your loved one and moving towards healing and forgiveness speaks volumes on your integrity.

Now the financial inventory. This is where you need to decide how you must handle finances from this point on. You must decide what is a zero tolerance for you and what you need to do to protect yourself should there be a relapse. I relapsed, and your loved one may too. Gambling is a horrible addiction and it had nothing to do with realizing I was hurting my loved ones.

Philippians 4:6-7. Recognize the things you can control; guard your peace. The world will continue to turn and spiral; protect your peace.

Identify some things that are zero tolerance?

_____

_____

_____

_____

_____

_____

_____

What can you do to protect yourself should there be a relapse?
What is the plan if that should occur?

_____

_____

_____

_____

_____

_____

_____

STEP 5

Admitted to ourselves and to another human being the exact nature of our wrongs.

DEAR LOVED ONE: It is hard to admit shame. We, by nature, are all prideful people. When your loved one gambled, it had nothing to do with deliberately hurting you. Very often, the gambler has convinced herself/himself that they are trying to better their situation, or trying to catch up to cover any losses. This is all part of the disease. Does that mean you were not hurt or betrayed. NO. Is an addiction an excuse or pardon for betrayal? NO.

I had a deep, deep fear of being caught and I protected my secrets more than anything. It was too hard to face that I was the rotten person doing the rotten things I had done while gambling. Even after coming clean to my loved ones, I even kept a few secrets to myself. I sometimes wonder if I was addicted to the secrets. It was a sense of control for me. There was a woman in GA who was a professional who was married to a catholic. She would show up at meetings twice a week having just come from the casino most times. Her husband was a catholic and divorce was not an option, so she would share how he took the hard-lined approach to their recovery, giving her no freedom whatsoever to work her recovery at her pace. Her recovery was miserable and she was in a marriage that seemed to have no hope for her. Boundaries have to be realistic or your loved one is never going to find respect to be a virtue of your relationship.

I don't have any advice other than to be patient. I know you want the truth and you want to know why. Each person's healing process is different. It is not always like a ripping off a bandaid and getting it over with. For some people, the truth may come out gradually because it is just, well, too painful. Also, the gambler's mind plays such tricks on rational thinking, that normal thoughts might take a while. The gambler may not honestly even remember.

In order to recover and restore your relationship, there must eventually be complete honesty. This is a tough step because the gambler has let dishonesty become a habit just like the gambling. There has to be an agreement that admitting all wrongdoings is safe. That you are not going to keep bringing up the past. Sometimes this means getting a counselor or pastoral ministry involved.

"Honesty is more than not lying. It is truth telling, truth speaking, truth living, and truth loving." "No legacy is so rich as honesty." "It takes strength and courage to admit the truth."

What are some questions you have for your loved one?

_____
_____
_____
_____
_____
_____
_____
_____
_____
_____
_____
_____
_____
_____
_____
_____
_____
_____
_____
_____
_____
_____
_____
_____

Will you be satisified with what the truth really is?

_____

_____

_____

_____

_____

_____

_____

_____

_____

_____

_____

_____

_____

_____

_____

_____

_____

_____

_____

_____

_____

_____

_____

_____

STEP 6

Were entirely ready to have these defects of character removed.

DEAR LOVED ONE: If your gambler is showing a true intent on working recovery, you will start to see changes. They want to be a better person. They know they are powerless over gambling. You will find that they ARE better person absent gambling, but do not forget that the defect is still there and relapse can occur because of merely just a tough day.

I have fallen off the wagon; more than once. I am an addict and I will always have this defect. I have found when I dabbled in gambling after entering recovery I thought I could handle it better this time around. I would be smarter this time. Again this is a lie. I ended up right back where I was and worse and trust had to start all over again. No-one says recovery is a permanent fix, and you must accept you are a human being and you are full of defects. We aren't striving for perfection. We strive to get through one day, and then a week, and then a month, etc. etc. Just like your loved one-you must pick yourself up and start over. This is where meeting must become a part of both of your lives. It is essential to recovery. You are always welcome at meetings to get a better understanding of the mind of a gambling addict, and the gambling addicts can also see the effect on their loved ones. I found that when people brought friends and loved ones to the meetings it ended up being very productive. Sometimes you can identify so much with the fellow gamblers but forget there are people in pain because of our gambling.

I know you probably don't want to hear this, but you are flawed as well, and you have defects. This is important when you are in pain, because when we are in pain we want to blame. Blaming will only halt recovery, and the goal is to conquer the steps. I had a friend who was in AA who said there were more miserable sober people at meetings than drunk people at the bar. Recovery is hard, but it is not meant to be miserable. Keep your eye on the HOPE of what can be.

Romans 12:12 ~ Rejoice in hope, be patient in tribulation, be constant in prayer.

John 8:7 Jesus says whoever is perfect, whoever has no sin, let him be the first one to throw a stone.

What are some of your own defects?

_____

_____

_____

_____

_____

_____

_____

_____

Do you see your loved on in your future?   What type of future can
you see?

_____

_____

_____

_____

_____

_____

_____

_____

_____

_____

STEP 7

Humbly asked God (of our understanding) to remove our shortcomings.

DEAD LOVED ONE: Not only is your gambler humbled, you are humbled as well. Just by working this journal you are willing to taking a leap of faith that God is going to work through you all and restore your relationship. We all have shortcomings.

It is funny how some people have shortcomings that we are willing to work through, but there are some we might feel are worthy of just being cut-off. A child, for instance, has tons of shortcomings. Their nature is to only thing of themselves, and if we would not set boundaries for them, they would eat whatever they want, sleep whenever they want, have poor manners, and behave however they want. We would never write off a child because we know there is hope to teach them, and guide them, and they will eventually mature. Obviouslly children are a work in progress as far as their morality goes and they are learning wrong from right. But aren't we all constantly learning? Gaining wisdom and knowledge? Last I checked, it does not just end when you are 18 years old. Or that there is no hope for you after a certain age.

Your gambler is looking at their entire life right now and identifying things that caused them to gamble. They are intently looking at their flaws and defects, and clinging to the hope that God will come through for them. They are banking on it.

I will never say that anything particularly caused me to gamble. I had choices and I made the wrong choices, and it was a downward spiral from there. I made a conscious decision not to focus too much on why, but to look forward and do better. Part of my own recovery was to look at myself like a child and that I was learning, and screwing up, and doing better, and GOD would never cut me off. It took me a long time to realize this, but when I did, my insecurities started to dissolve.

My husband had friends who gave him all kinds of advice that they would leave, and they couldn't forgive, etc. But he loved me and could not see his life or future without me. I hurt him and it still hurts me to think about it too much.

Unlike defects, shortcomings are our weaknesses. How do you strengthen a weakness? To build up strength. To repeat and repeat and repeat. Sometimes people mistake weaknesses for anxiety. They have such an intense fear of something that they run the other way. Don't run. Don't give up. As long as we have weaknesses there is hope to make them strong.

"My grace is sufficient for you, for my power is made perfect in weakness."

Identify your own weaknesses. Identify your loved-ones weaknesses.

_____

_____

_____

_____

_____

_____

_____

_____

Write a letter to God about being your strength where you are weak.

STEP 8

Made a list of all persons we had harmed and became willing to make amends to them all.

DEAR LOVED ONE: You were harmed. You are on the list. You may be the first person on the list. Your loved one is figuring out how to make amends to you. Only you are on the only one who knows what that is. It may be money. It may be trust. It may be control. It is important for you to communicate in a loving way what you need for healing, and what they need to do. This must be clear so if you are not sure, you may need to spend some prayer and meditation on this. Clear communication about what you need may prevent a relapse.

Needs and wants are something entirely different. Our needs are real. Our wants may not be attainable. Recovery has to be attainable. Not necessarily easy, but attainable.

Philippians 4:19 tells us that God will supply our needs, but He never promised to meet all our wants. The truth is, even getting our "wants" will not necessarily make us happy.

What are your needs in your relationship?

_____
_____
_____
_____
_____
_____
_____
_____

What are your wants in your relationship?

_____
_____
_____
_____
_____

If your loved one is ready to share how he is willing to make amends, how do your lists compare?

_____
_____
_____
_____
_____

STEP 9

Make direct amends to such people wherever possible, except when to do so would injure them or others.

DEAR LOVED ONE: Your gambler may have quite a bit of work to do on this step, so this may take a while. Be ready to be patient. Be also ready to understand that there are more people on that list than you.

My list was pages long. I had become so manipulative when I was gambling, that I lied just because I had no idea how to tell the truth. I lied about stuff that didn't even matter if I told the truth. I don't know if I ever made proper amends to most of those people. I think I even left a lot of people off the list because I just didn't remember.

People are often confused about the harm/injure part of this step. Sometimes reparations can be made subtly without blowing up your future. For instance, there was a woman who had stolen money from her child's bank account. She was in recovery and wanted to make amends to her child. She put every penny and more of that money back in the bank account without telling her child what she had actually done. She was able to repair that injury to her child without damaging their relationship further. Recovery is tough and there are things that may be too harmful to proceeding. The key is to stop gambling. I know people who have worked on this step for years waiting for the right time.

Reparations Include Five Key Components:

Cessation/Assurance of Non-Repetition,

Restitution and Repatriation,

Compensation,

Satisfaction, and

Rehabilitation.

Do you have any fears about things you are not ready for?

_____

_____

_____

_____

_____

_____

_____

_____

Are you satisfied with your loved-ones reparations? Are there reparations that are a one time fix, or some that are life-long?

_____

_____

_____

_____

_____

_____

_____

_____

_____

STEP 10

Continued to take personal inventory and when we were wrong, promptly admitted it.

DEAR LOVED ONE: If your loved one relapses what will you do? How do you plan to hold that person accountable?

Have you ever watched the show *Intervention*? The family all confront the addict and give them an ultimatum to going into rehab. It seems about 50/50 that people actually recover this way because some reluctantly go. This may be the case with your loved one. Were they forced into recovery? Do they still have a relationship with their addiction? Is their recovery miserable because the thrill of gambling is all they enjoyed? The truth is, you don't have the power to make your loved one do anything. They have to choose themselves. All you can do is protect yourself, and if it comes to a point where they are not recovering, you have to make a choice. I won't lie. Relapses happen and they suck. It's like starting all over. However, your gambler is learning how to stop the compulsion in its tracks.

One person at GA meetings had been in recovery for years but had stopped going to meetings. He started coming to meetings again because he had gone into a casino but turned around and walked out before betting anything and headed straight to a meeting that day. He had developed tools to stop a relapse, and one of those tools is the meetings and take things one day at a time.

You too can take things one day at a time. You are the only one who know what you need and how to be fulfilled.

"No matter what happens today, I can handle it."

Have you set any boundaries on relapses?   Are there tools set in place to know your loved one is being honest?

_____

_____

_____

_____

_____

_____

_____

_____

Without focusing on the relapse, are their things that are better with your love-ones behavior? Your relationship?

_____

_____

_____

_____

_____

_____

_____

STEP 11

Sought through prayer and meditation to improve our conscious contact with God as we understood Him, praying only for knowledge of His will for us and the power to carry that out.

DEAR LOVED ONE: God's will is to have eternal life for everyone. God's will is for you to prosper. God's will is for you to have peace in your life. Sometimes it is so easy for us to tell God how we want to obtain those things. Sometimes we don't know if we are even going to like God's will. Life is just a journey and we are all *limping to Jerusalem*, and sometimes people need help getting there.

I suggest you look back in your notebook and pull the scripture quotes in your bible. This book is not necessarily a bible study, but focuses on steps that will get you to a more trusting relationship with God. I guarantee you will find peace in reading about God's forgiveness and mercy, and casting stones, and troubles and worry. He has it handled. Let him handle it. Meditate on peace. Meditate on recovery. Meditate on restoration (financially and mentally). It will manifest I promise. It may be on God's time, but his time is perfect.

Philippians 4:6-7 *Do not be anxious about anything, but in every situation, by prayer and petition, with thanksgiving, present your requests to God.*

What things in your life bring you peace and joy?

_____

_____

_____

_____

_____

_____

_____

_____

What things in your life bring you stress and chaos?

_____

_____

_____

_____

_____

STEP 12

Having made an effort to practice these principles in all our affairs, we tried to carry this message to other compulsive gamblers.

DEAR LOVED ONE: Are you ready to talk to others about your journey with loving a compulsive gambler. There are so many people who are affected by various addicts, and it is not easy. It takes courage to be knocked down and get back up, and even harder to help pick someone else up too. You will be surprised once you start talking about it, how people will open up to you. One of the reasons I authored this book (along with my husband) is because I started owning my addiction and I had people remember that and come to me when they had a similar problem. Without bragging, I have had success with talking people off their ledge and they went on to live very fulfilled lives despite their flaws and shortcomings. I realize not ever story is the same. I am also not hear to tell you it's all easy. It isn't. My husband and I had horrible fights and brought up past hurts and mistakes many times. There is such a shame associated with addictions and it is so hard to recover from it. We all need to be understanding, compassionate, aware of our own needs, aware of other needs, yet try to act righteous ourselves. It's exhausting isn't it? But hardships can bring us closer together and closer to God. So, the bottom line is it all comes down to love. Maybe we CAN all just be broken together.

In order to repair and preserve the house, you must get down to clean, sound wood. You must search out and destroy all the weak, rotted, crumbling wood wherever you find it.

What changes have you seen in yourself during these 12 steps?

_____

_____

_____

_____

_____

_____

_____

What has changed in your relationship for the better?

_____

_____

_____

_____

_____

What are you thankful for today?

_____
_____
_____
_____
_____
_____
_____
_____
_____
_____
_____
_____
_____

How do you see your life in 10 years?

_____
_____
_____
_____
_____
_____
_____
_____
_____
_____
_____

BROKEN TOGETHER

What do you think about when you look at me?
I know we're not the fairytale you dreamed we'd be
You wore the veil, you walked the aisle, you took my hand
And we dove into a mystery
How I wish we could go back to simpler times
Before all our scars and all our secrets were in the light
Now on this hallowed ground, we've drawn the battle lines
Will we make it through the night?
It's going to take much more than promises this time
Only God can change our minds
Maybe you and I were never meant to be complete
Could we just be broken together?
If you can bring your shattered dreams and I'll bring mine
Could healing still be spoken and save us?
The only way we'll last forever is broken together
How it must have been so lonely by my side
We were building kingdoms
And chasing dreams and left love behind
I'm praying God will help our broken hearts align
And we won't give up the fight
It's going to take much more than promises this time
Only God can change our minds
Maybe you and I were never meant to be complete
Could we just be broken together?
If you can bring your shattered dreams, and I'll bring mine
Could healing still be spoken and save us?
The only way we'll last forever is broken together
Maybe you and I were never meant to be complete
Could we just be broken together?

Casting Crowns- Bernie
Herms / John Mark Hall

Extra Pages to Journal

HELPFUL SITES

https://www.gamblersanonymous.org/ga

National Helpline 1-800-GAMBLER

Dial: 988 (Mental Health Assistance)

https://gasteps.org/free-literature-downloads

Made in the USA
Las Vegas, NV
08 January 2024

84100357R00026